SHAKESPEARE FOR

HAML

HENRY THE FIFTH

JULIUS CAESAR

MACBETH

A MIDSUMMER NIGHT'S DREAM

MUCH ADO ABOUT NOTHING

ROMEO AND JULIET

THE TAMING OF THE SHREW

THE TEMPEST

TWELFTH NIGHT

SHAKESPEARE ON STAGE

AS YOU LIKE IT

HAMLET

JULIUS CAESAR

MACBETH

THE MERCHANT OF VENICE

A MIDSUMMER NIGHT'S DREAM

OTHELLO, THE MOOR OF VENICE

ROMEO AND JULIET

Juliet: (To herself) O Romeo, Romeo! Wherefore art thou "Romeo"?

SHAKESPEARE FOR YOUNG PEOPLE

ROMEO AND JULIET

by
William Shakespeare

edited and illustrated by
Diane Davidson

SWAN BOOKS
A division of Learning Links Inc.
New Hyde Park, New York

Published by:

SWAN BOOKS
a division of:
LEARNING LINKS INC.
2300 Marcus Avenue
New Hyde Park, NY 11042

Printed in the United States of America

Library of Congress Cataloging-in-Publication Data

Shakespeare, William, 1564–1616.
  Romeo and Juliet for young people.

  (Shakespeare for young people)
  Summary: An abridged version of Shakespeare's original text, with suggestions for simple staging. Includes
parenthetical explanations and descriptions within the
text and announcers who summarize deleted passages.
ISBN 0-7675-0841-6 (pbk.)
  1. Children's plays, English. [1. Plays]
I. Davidson, Diane. II. Title. III. Series:
Shakespeare, William, 1564–1616. Shakespeare for
young people
PR2831.A25 1986   822.3'3   86–5958

TO THE TEACHER OR PARENT

Young people can grow up loving Shakespeare if they act out his plays. Since Shakespeare wrote for the theater, not for the printed page, he is most exciting on his own ground.

Many people are afraid that the young will not understand Shakespeare's words. To help these actors follow the story, the editor has added two optional announcers, who introduce and explain the scenes. However, young people pick up the general meaning with surprising ease, and they enjoy the words without completely understanding them at first. Their ears tell them the phrases often sound like music, and the plays are full of marvelous scenes.

After all, Shakespeare is not called the best of all writers because he is hard. He is the best of all writers because he is enjoyable!

HOW TO BEGIN

At first, students may find the script too difficult to enjoy, so one way to start is for the director to read the play aloud. Between scenes, he can ask, "What do you think is going to happen next?" or "Do you think the character should do this?" After the students become familiar with the story and words, they can try out for parts by reading different scenes. In the end, the director should pick the actors he thinks are best, emphasizing, "There are no small parts. Everybody helps in a production."

The plays can be presented in several ways.

In the simplest form, the students can read the script aloud, sitting in their seats. This will do well enough, but it is more fun to put on the actual show.

What can a director do to help his actors?

One main point in directing is to have the actors speak the words loudly and clearly. It helps if they speak a little

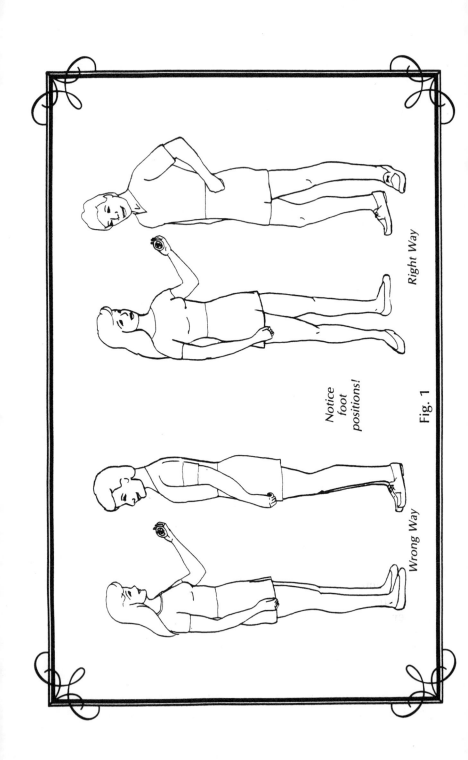

Right Way

Notice foot positions!

Wrong Way

Fig. 1

more slowly than usual. They should not be afraid to pause or to emphasize short phrases. However, they should not try to be "arty" or stilted. Shakespeare wrote very energetic plays.

A second main point in directing is to keep the students facing the audience, even if they are talking to someone else. They should "fake front," so that their bodies face the audience and their heads are only half-way towards the other actors. (Fig. 1)

The cast should be told that when the announcers speak between scenes, servants can continue to change the stage set, and actors can enter, exit, or stand around pretending to talk silently. But if an announcer speaks during a scene, the actors should "freeze" until the announcer has finished his lines. At no time should the actors look at the announcers. (The announcers' parts may be cut out if the director so desires.)

Encouragement and applause inspire the young to do better, and criticism should always be linked with a compliment. Often, letting the students find their own way through the play produces the best results. And telling them, "Mean what you say," or "Be more energetic!" is all they really need.

SCHEDULES AND BUDGET

Forty-five minutes a day—using half the time for group scenes and half the time for individual scenes—is generally enough for students to rehearse. The director should encourage all to learn their lines as soon as possible. An easy way to memorize lines is to tape them and have the student listen to the tape at home each evening, going over it four or five times. Usually actors learn faster by ear than by eye. In all, it takes about six weeks to prepare a good show.

The play seems more complete if it has an audience, even other people from next door. But an afternoon or evening

public performance is better yet. The director should an-
nounce the show well in advance. A PTA meeting, Open
House, a Renaissance Fair, a holiday—all are excellent
times to do a play.

To attract a good crowd, the admission should be very
small or free. However, a Drama Fund is always useful, so
some groups pass a hat, or parents sell cookies and punch.
But the best way to raise money for a Drama Fund is to
sell advertising in the program. A business-card size ad
can sell for $5 to $10, and a larger ad can bring in even
more. This money can be used for costumes or small 250-
500 watt spotlights. Until there is money in the Drama
Fund, the director often becomes an expert at borrowing
and improvising. Fortunately, Shakespeare's plays can be
produced with almot no scenery or special costumes, and
there are no royalties to pay.

SPECIAL NOTES ON THIS PLAY

Romeo and Juliet needs only simple staging: two "wings"
or screens on each side of the stage area, and a curtained
alcove across the back. If the school has a stage, fine. But
good shows can take place at one end of a room.

What can people use as screens? Tall cardboard refriger-
ator boxes are good. Stage flats, frames of 1" x 4" lumber
joined by triangles of plywood and covered with muslin
sheeting, are excellent if little side flats are hinged to the
main one to provide bracing. The curtain across the back
is necessary for Juliet's bed and her tomb, both using the
same cot. Three six- or eight-foot ladders can make the
basis for the alcove. A pole between the ladders will sup-
port curtains made of two sheets, especially if the ladders
are weighted with buckets of bricks to keep them from
tipping over. Two additional sheets hide the ladders, and a

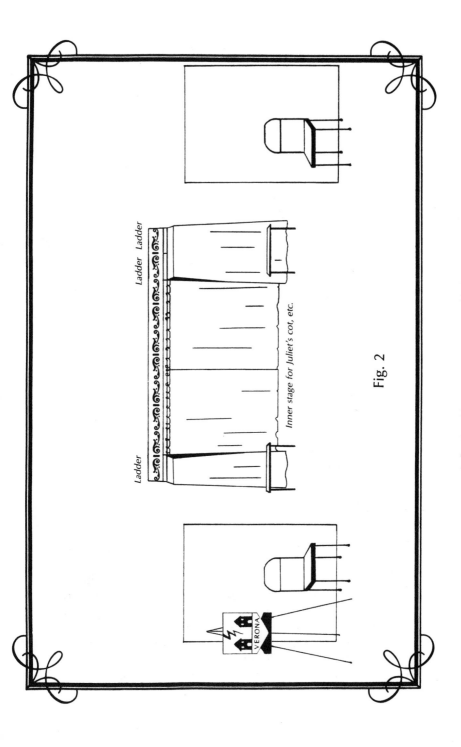

Ladder Ladder

Ladder

Inner stage for Juliet's cot, etc.

VERONA

Fig. 2

decorative cardboard header gives a finished look. Aluminum duct tape holds the sheets and cardboard best. The ladders double as balcony elevations. Two of the ladders should be together, as Romeo appears with Juliet in the second balcony scene. Benches on each side of the alcove complete the scenery. (Fig. 2)

This play has so many settings that banners can indicate the different scenes. A servant can hang a banner on a screen or easel, changing it when necessary. Some suggested designs are shown in Fig. 3.

On each side of the stage there should be chairs where the two announcers sit during the scenes.

Romeo and Juliet is usually performed in medieval or Renaissance costumes. Draperies make excellent material, often donated by thrift shops or dry cleaners with unclaimed goods. Players who portray older men wear dark full-length robes that are richly trimmed. Younger men and servants wear short pants with bare legs or tights, plus full blouses (ladies' blouses, belted, with sleeves puffed by several elastic bands, do very well). The party masks can be fantastic shapes sprayed with gold paint. The Prince should wear a crown. Ladies wear dresses with long sleeves and full-length skirts. Juliet often wears a little pearl cap. Older women wear veils or jeweled headbands. To help the audience understand the plot, it is good for all Capulets to wear one color (perhaps cream) while Montagues wear another color (blue) and the Prince, Mercutio and Paris a third (purple).

A word of warning is necessary: all sword-fights should be carefully rehearsed, with much waving of swords at a distance and little actual combat. Students should be very careful not to play with even imitation swords or daggers, as someone may be hurt.

For background music, a fine choice would be Tchiakovsky's *Romeo and Juliet Overture* or Elizabethan music.

BANNERS

Verona

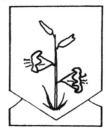

Juliet's Chamber

Capulet's House

Juliet's Balcony

Friar's Cell

Mantua

Juliet's Tomb

Fig. 3

A LAST BIT OF ADVICE

How will a director know if he has produced Shakespeare "correctly"? He should ask his group if they had fun. If they answer, "Yes," then the show is a success!

CHARACTERS

Two Announcers (optional), who have been added

The Royal Family
Escalus (**Es**-ca-lus), Prince of Verona
Mercutio (Mer-**kew**-shee-oh), the Prince's clever
cousin and Romeo's good friend
Paris, the Prince's cousin and Juliet's fiance
Page, servant to Paris

The House of Montague
Montague (**Mont**-uh-gew), an old nobleman
Lady Montague, his wife
Romeo, their romantic young son
Benvolio (Ben-**vol**-ee-oh), Romeo's sensible cousin
Balthasar (**Bal**-tha-sar) and Abraham, servants

The House of Capulet
Old Capulet (**Cap**-u-let), an energetic father
Lady Capulet, his young sophisticated wife
Juliet, their lovely daughter, age thirteen
Tybalt (**Tib**-alt), Capulet's hot-tempered nephew
Nurse, Juliet's jolly servant
Peter, a stupid servant
Sampson and Gregory, servants

Others
Friar Lawrence, a kindly old priest
Apothecary (A-**poth**-i-cary) a medieval druggist
Officer and Watchmen, local police
Citizens, Gentlemen, Ladies, and Servants

ACT I

(The Verona banner indicates the scenery. The two announcers enter, bow and take their places on each side of the stage area.)

Announcer 1: (To the audience) Welcome, everyone, to a production of Shakespeare's *Romeo and Juliet* given by the _____ class.

Announcer 2: This is not the complete play but a very short edition for young people, using the original words.

Announcer 1: We two announcers have been added to the play to help explain any hard parts.

Announcer 2: You will notice some long words, because in Shakespeare's time, people liked to play with long words as a sort of game with sounds.

Announcer 1: The story begins, "In fair Verona, where we lay our scene." Here in beautiful Italy, two rich families are deadly enemies. The families are named Montague and Capulet.

Announcer 2: Romeo, the son of the Montagues, falls in love with Juliet, the daughter of the Capulets.

Announcer 1: In those days, people thought luck depended on their horoscope and stars. Since Romeo and Juliet were unlucky, they are called the "star-crossed lovers."

Announcer 2: The action starts with a street-fight between servants of the two families. And the Prince of Verona becomes very angry.

(The announcers sit at each side, as two servants of the Capulets, big Sampson and little Gregory, stroll onstage. They see Abraham and Balthasar, two servants of the Montagues.)

Gregory: (To Sampson) Draw thy tool! Here comes two of the house of the Montagues.

Sampson: (Waving his sword weakly.) My naked weapon is out. *(He pushes little Gregory towards the others.)* Quarrel! I . . . will back thee!

Gregory: How? Turn thy back and run? *(He tries to hide behind big Sampson.)*

Sampson: (Mischievously) I will bite my thumb at them. *(He strolls up to the Montague servants and bites his thumb at them. They grab him roughly.)*

Abraham: Do you bite your thumb at us, sir?

Sampson: (Innocently) I do bite my thumb.

Abraham: (Roughly) Do you bite your thumb at us, sir?

Sampson: (Weakly) No, sir, I do not bite my thumb at you, sir. *(They let him go.)* But I bite my thumb, sir! *(They seize him again.)*

Gregory: (Looking offstage towards Tybalt) Here comes one of my master's kinsmen!

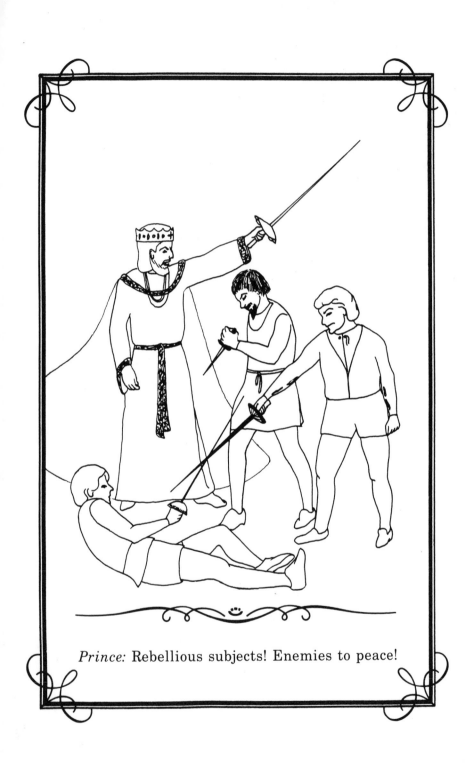

Prince: Rebellious subjects! Enemies to peace!

Sampson: (Struggling free and egging the Montagues to fight.) Draw, if you be men! *(To his friend)* Gregory, remember thy swashing blow!

(Others enter and join the fight—kind Benvolio, of the Montagues, and proud Tybalt, of the Capulets. Also Lord and Lady Montague and Lord and Lady Capulet enter, though they do not fight. The shouts bring out the Prince, who commands all to stop. But the fighters do not listen at first.)

Prince: Rebellious subjects! Enemies to peace! . . . Will they not hear? . . . What, ho! You men, you beasts! *(The crowd begins to quiet.)* On pain of torture, from those bloody hands throw your weapons to the ground, and hear the sentence of your moved Prince! *(The people drop their swords, ashamed.)*

Announcer 1: The Prince announces that, from now on, all street fighting will be punished by death.

Prince: (Speaking to the two old noblemen.) Three brawls, old Capulet and Montague, have thrice disturbed the quiet of our streets. *(To all)* If ever you disturb our streets again, your lives shall pay the forfeit of the peace! *(The crowd gasps.)* For this time, on pain of death, all men depart! *(All leave except Benvolio, who shakes his head thoughtfully. Romeo enters, looking sad.)*

Announcer 2: A young man who has not been fighting is Romeo, a Montague. He is in love with a girl named Rosaline, but she is not in love with him.

Benvolio: (To Romeo) Good morrow, cousin!

Romeo: Ay, me! Sad hours seem long. *(They sit down.)*

Benvolio: Tell me in sadness, who is that you love?

Romeo: In sadness, cousin, I do love . . . a woman!

Benvolio: (Grinning) I aimed so near when I supposed you loved.

Romeo: (Explaining the girl will not love him back.) She'll not be hit with Cupid's arrow.

Benvolio: (As some pretty girls run by, laughing.) Examine other beauties.

Romeo: Thou canst not teach me to forget. *(He sighs.)*

Announcer 1: A servant of the enemy house of Capulet appears with a list of people to invite to a feast. Unfortunately, he cannot read.

Peter: (Entering, he scratches his head. Then he smiles at Romeo.) I pray, sir, can you read?

Romeo: Ay, if I know the letters and the language. *(He takes the list and starts reading.)* "Signior Martino and his wife and daughters. County Anselme and his beauteous sisters. *(Benvolio whistles and grins.)* The lady widow of Vitruvio. *(All three make sour faces.)* Signior Placentio and his lovely nieces. Mercutio and his brother Valentine. Mine uncle Capulet, his wife and daughters. My fair niece Rosaline! *(Romeo stops and sighs. Benvolio points to the name, and Romeo nods. It is his love.)* A fair assembly. Whither should they come?

Peter: Up! To supper. To our house. *(He grins.)*

Romeo: Whose house? *(He returns the list.)*

Peter: Now I'll tell you. My master is the great rich Capulet. And if you be not of the house of Montagues, I pray come and crush a cup of wine! *(He bows as he leaves.)* Rest you merry!

Benvolio: (Excited) At this same feast of Capulet's sups the fair Rosaline, whom thou so lovest. Go, and compare her face with some that I shall show. And I will make thee think thy "swan" a crow!

Romeo: (He laughs at the idea) One fairer than my love? *(But he shrugs and agrees.)* I'll go along, no such sight to be shown, but to rejoice in splendor of mine own. *(They leave.)*

(A servant enters, putting up a banner for Juliet's room. The Nurse comes and sits, sewing. Lady Capulet enters from the other side.)

Announcer 2: So Benvolio and Romeo plan to go to the Capulet's feast to compare his love Rosaline with other girls. Meanwhile, Lady Capulet comes to the room of her daughter Juliet. It seems a nice young count named Paris wants to marry the girl.

Lady Capulet: Nurse, where's my daughter?

Nurse: (Going to the side of the stage.) What, lamb! What, ladybird! *(To herself, crossly)* God forbid, where's this girl? *(Calls louder)* What, Ju-li-et!

Juliet: (Entering in a lovely white gown, she runs and kneels before her mother.) Madam, I am here. What is your will?

Lady Capulet: This is the matter . . . *(She waves the Nurse away.)* Nurse, give leave awhile. We must talk in secret. *(The Nurse goes away, sulking. Lady Capulet changes her mind.)* Nurse, come back again. *(The Nurse returns, smiling. They all sit, as Lady Capulet speaks to the Nurse.)* Thou knowest my daughter's of a pretty age.

Nurse: Come Lammas Eve at night shall she be fourteen. *(She kisses Juliet.)* Thou wast the prettiest babe that e'er I nursed. An I might live to see thee married once, I have my wish.

Lady Capulet: Marry, that "marry" is the very theme I came to talk of. Tell me, daughter Juliet, how stands your disposition to be married?

Juliet: (Shyly) It is an honor that I dream not of.

Lady Capulet: (Rising and taking the girl's hand so she also rises.) Well, think of marriage now. In brief, the valiant Paris seeks you for his love!

Nurse: (Throwing up her hands at so excellent a husband.) A man, young lady . . . why, he's a man of wax! He's a flower, in faith . . . a very flower!

Lady Capulet: (To Juliet) What say you? Can you love the gentleman? *(Juliet shrugs, uncertain.)* This night you shall behold him at our feast!

Juliet: (Obediently) I'll look to like.

Peter: (Entering in a hurry) Madam, the guests are come, supper served up, you called, my young lady asked for, the Nurse cursed in the pantry, and everything in extremity! I beseech you, follow straight! *(He dashes out again. The women laugh.)*

Lady Capulet: We follow thee! *(They all leave.)*

(While a servant changes the banner to Verona's streets, Romeo, Benvolio and fun-loving Mercutio enter with a torch and masks.)

Announcer 1: In those days, fashionable bachelors could go to feasts without invitations. They would wear masks and dance with all the ladies.

Mercutio: Nay, gentle Romeo, we must have you dance!

Romeo: (Sadly) Not I, believe me. You have dancing shoes with nimble soles. I have a soul of lead. A torch for me! I'll be a candleholder and look on. *(He takes the torch and adds thoughtfully.)* I dreamt a dream tonight.

Mercutio: (Grinning) And so did I!

Romeo: Well, what was yours?

Mercutio: That dreamers often lie . . .

Romeo: . . . in bed asleep, while they do dream things true.

Announcer 2: Mercutio, to cheer up Romeo, gives a fantastic description of the dream-fairy, Queen Mab, who visits lovers.

Announcer 1: She is as tiny as the jewel in a ring, and her little coach is made of insect parts.

Mercutio: O, then I see Queen Mab hath been with you! She is the fairies' midwife. And she comes in shape no bigger than an agate stone, drawn with a team of little atomies athwart men's noses as they lie asleep. Her wagon spokes made of long spinners' legs; the cover, of the wings of grasshoppers; her collars, of the moonshine's watery beams; her whip of cricket's bone. Her chariot is an empty hazel-nut made by the joiner squirrel, time out of mind the fairies' coach-makers. And in this state she gallops night by night through lovers' brains, and then they dream of . . . LOVE! *(He makes a silly face.)*

Romeo: (Smiling in spite of himself.) Peace, peace, Mercutio, peace! Thou talkest of nothing!

Benvolio: Supper is done, and we shall come too late.

Romeo: (Strangely) I fear too early. *(But he and the others put on their masks.)*

(Servants put up Capulet's banner. Music plays. Some guests and Capulet enter and dance in a graceful circle. Juliet and her mother enter with the Nurse. Romeo and his friends stand and watch.)

Capulet: (To the masked bachelors.) Welcome, gentlemen! *(To the ladies)* Ah ha, my mistresses, which of you all will now deny to dance? She that makes dainty . . . she, I'll swear, hath corns! *(All laugh, and Capulet bustles about, being the jolly host.)*

Announcer 2: But at the feast, instead of finding his Rosaline, Romeo falls in love with Juliet.

(Juliet dances with Paris while Romeo stares at her more and more.)

Announcer 1: A quick-tempered Capulet cousin, Tybalt, recognizes Romeo and wants to kill him for coming to their house.

Tybalt: (To a page, angrily) Fetch me my rapier, boy!

Capulet: (Joining Tybalt) Why, kinsman, wherefore storm you so?

Tybalt: (Pointing to Romeo) Uncle, this is a Montague, our foe!

Capulet: (Looking closely) Young Romeo, is it?

Tybalt: 'Tis he, that villain Romeo!

Capulet: (Quietly) Let him alone. And, to say truth,

Verona brags of him to be a virtuous and well-governed youth. Take no note of him.

Tybalt: (Furious) I'll not endure him!

Capulet: Go to! You are a saucy boy! *(Smiling, to his guests)* Well said, my hearts! *(Angrily to Tybalt)* You are a princox, go! Be quiet, or . . . *(To the servants)* More light, more light! *(To Tybalt!)* For shame! I'll make you quiet! *(To the guests)* Cheerly, my hearts! *(He pushes Tybalt away and joins the guests. Tybalt leaves.)*

(Romeo steps into the dance and leads Juliet to one side of the stage, where he holds her hand.)

Announcer 2: Romance in these times often began by putting the girl on a pedestal, high above the young man.

Announcer 1: So Romeo pretends that Juliet is a holy saint, and he is a pilgrim who worships at the shrine of her hand.

Romeo: If I profane with my unworthiest hand this holy shrine, the gentle fine is this: my lips, two blushing pilgrims, ready stand, to smooth that rough touch with a tender kiss. *(He kisses the palm of her hand. She smiles with delight.)*

Juliet: (Protesting he shows good manners.) Good Pilgrim, you do wrong your hand too much, which mannerly devotion shows in this. For saints have hands that pilgrims' hands do touch. *(She slides*

Juliet and Count Paris

her hand into his, matching palms.) And palm-to-palm is holy palmer's kiss!

Romeo: (Coming closer) Have not saints lips, and holy palmers too?

Juliet: Ay, Pilgrim, lips that they must use in prayer.

Romeo: O then, Dear Saint, let lips do what hands do! *(He kisses her lightly.)*

Juliet: (Laughing) You kiss, by the Book! *(But the Nurse hurries over to separate them.)*

Nurse: Madam, your mother craves a word with you! *(Juliet curtsies to Romeo and leaves.)*

Romeo: (To the Nurse) What is her mother?

Nurse: (Proudly and happily) Marry, bachelor, her mother is the lady of the house! *(She follows Juliet. The guests start to leave.)*

Romeo: (To himself, shocked) Is she a Capulet?

Capulet: (Trying to get the guests to stay a little.) Nay, gentlemen, prepare not to be gone! *(But Romeo and his friends go to the door. Capulet goes with them, the smiling host.)*

Juliet: Come hither, Nurse. What's he that follows there, that would not dance? *(She points to Romeo.)*

Nurse: I know not. *(She whispers to a guest and returns with a serious look.)* His name is Romeo, and a Montague, the only son of your great enemy!

Juliet: *(To herself, shocked)* My only love, sprung from my only hate!

Nurse: Come, let's away. The strangers all are gone. *(Juliet exits slowly, looking back as she goes.)*

ACT II

Announcer 2: So Juliet, a Capulet, and Romeo, a Montague, fall in love in spite of their families.

(As a servant brings on a street banner, Romeo runs in and hides. Benvolio and Mercutio enter laughing.)

Benvolio: (Calling) Romeo! My cousin Romeo! Ro-me-o!

Mercutio: (Yawning) He hath stolen him home to bed!

Benvolio: Call, good Mercutio!

Mercutio: (Full of fun, he draws his sword and waves it like a magician's wand.) Romeo! Madman! Lover! Appear thou! Speak but one rhyme and I am satisfied. Pronounce but "love" and "dove"! *(He looks around and shrugs.)* He heareth not, he stirreth not, he moveth not. The ape is dead! *(Calling)* Romeo—good night!

(They leave, laughing, as the orchard banner is put in place. Romeo comes out of hiding. Juliet climbs a ladder so she appears to be on a balcony above him.)

Announcer 1: Romeo, hoping to see Juliet again, climbs over the wall into the Capulet's garden.

Romeo: (Looking up to see Juliet. In her white dress, she looks like sunlight.) But soft, what light through yonder window breaks? It is the east, and Juliet is the sun! It is my lady! O, it is my love!

Juliet: (Resting her cheek on her hand, she gazes at the moon.) Ay, me . . .

Romeo: (To himself) She speaks! O speak again, Bright Angel!

Announcer 2: Juliet wishes Romeo had another name, so he would not be a Montague, an enemy.

Juliet: (To herself) O Romeo, Romeo! Wherefore art thou "Romeo"? What's in a name? That which we call a "rose" by any other name would smell as sweet.

Romeo: (Standing where she can see him, he calls up to her.) Call me but "Love" and I'll be new-baptized. Henceforth I never will be "Romeo"!

Juliet: (At first startled and then happy.) Art thou not Romeo? And a Montague?

Romeo: (Smiling) Neither, Fair Saint, if either thee dislike.

Juliet: How camest thou hither? The orchard walls are high and hard to climb! *(With fear)* And the place death, if any of my kinsmen find thee here. If they do see thee, they will murder thee!

Romeo: I have night's cloak to hide me from their sight.

Juliet: (Seriously) Dost thou love me? I know thou wilt say, "Ay," and I will take thy word. O gentle Romeo, if thou dost love, pronounce it faithfully!

Romeo: (Raising his hand to swear an oath.) Lady, by yonder blessed moon I swear, that tips with silver all these fruit-tree tops . . .

Juliet: (Interrupting) O swear not by the moon, that monthly changes in her circled orb.

Romeo: What shall I swear by?

Juliet: Do not swear at all. *(She blows him a kiss.)* Sweet, good night.

Nurse: (Offstage) Juliet, Juliet!

Juliet: (To the Nurse) Anon! *(To Romeo)* Stay but a little. I will come again. *(She leaves.)*

Romeo: (To himself) O blessed, blessed night! I am afeard all this is but a dream.

Announcer 1: When Juliet returns, she proposes marriage to Romeo.

Announcer 2: And she promises to send a messenger to him to make wedding arrangements.

Juliet: (Appearing again on her balcony) Dear Romeo! If that thy bent of love be honorable, thy purpose marriage, send me word tomorrow by one that I'll procure to come to thee!

Nurse: (Calling in a cross voice) Madam!

Juliet: (Calling back) By and by I come! *(To Romeo)* Tomorrow will I send. *(She leaves again.)*

Romeo: How silver-sweet sound lovers' tongues by night, like softest music to attending ears!

Juliet: (Returning) Romeo . . .

Romeo: My dear?

Juliet: At what o'clock tomorrow shall I send to thee?

Romeo: At the hour of nine.

Juliet: I will not fail. 'Tis twenty years till then. *(They fall silent, looking at each other, until Juliet laughs in embarrassment.)* I have forgot why I did call thee back.

Romeo: Let me stand here till thou remember it.

Juliet: I shall forget, to have thee still stand there, remembering how I love thy company.

Romeo: And I'll still stay, to have thee still forget! *(They laugh together.)*

Juliet: (Looking at the sky) 'Tis almost morning. *(She leaves slowly.)* Good night, good night! Parting is such sweet sorrow that I shall say, "Good night," till it be morrow!

Romeo: (As she leaves) Sleep dwell upon thine eyes, peace in thy breast! *(He gazes after her.)*

Announcer 1: Romeo decides to visit his priest and counselor, old Friar Lawrence, for help.

Romeo: (With decision) Hence will I to my ghostly father's cell, his help to crave and my dear hap to tell! *(He leaves joyously.)*

Announcer 2: As morning dawns, the old friar collects herbs and flowers to make medicine.

(A servant brings on herbs and the banner with a cross. The Friar enters, carrying a basket.)

Friar: The gray-eyed morn smiles on the frowning night, checkering the eastern clouds with streaks of light. Now, I must up-fill this osier-cage of ours with baleful weeds and precious-juiced flowers. *(He goes about, picking herbs.)* Many for many virtues excellent, none but for some, and yet . . . all different!

(Picking up a flower) Within the infant rind of this small flower, poison hath residence and medicine power. For this, being smelt, with that part cheers each part. Being tasted, slays all senses with the heart. *(He shakes his head with wonder that something is both good and bad.)*

Romeo: (Entering) Good morrow, Father!

Friar: (With a smile) Young son, where hast thou been?

Romeo: (Mysteriously) I have been feasting with mine enemy, where, on a sudden, one hath wounded me that's by me wounded!

Friar: (Frowning) Be plain, good son!

Romeo: (Smiling) Then . . . plainly know my heart's dear love is set on the fair daughter of rich Capulet! This I pray . . . that thou consent to marry us today!

Friar: (Putting down his basket in surprise) Holy Saint Francis, what a change is here! Is Rosaline so soon forsaken? *(Romeo looks embarrassed. The Friar chuckles.)* But come, young waverer, come go with me. In one respect, I'll thy assistant be.

Announcer 1: The old priest agrees to help the lovers, in the hope that their marriage will stop the family quarrel.

Friar: For this alliance may so happy prove, to turn your households' rancor to pure love.

Romeo: (Pulling his arm to make him hurry.) O, let us hence! I stand on sudden haste!

Friar: (Slowing him down) Wisely and slow! They stumble that run fast! *(He takes his basket.)*

(As Romeo drags the Friar off, a servant brings Juliet's banner. Juliet enters impatiently.)

Announcer 2: A little later, Juliet waits for the Nurse to return from seeing Romeo about wedding plans.

Juliet: The clock struck nine when I did send the Nurse. In half an hour she promised to return. Perchance she cannot meet him! . . . That's not so. O, she is lame. *(She sees the Nurse hobble in, very tired.)* O honey Nurse, what news?

Nurse: (To tease her, she pretends she is too tired to speak.) I am aweary. Fie, how my bones ache!

Juliet: Nay, come, I pray thee, speak!

Nurse: What haste! Do you not see that I am out of breath?

Juliet: (Too eagerly) How art thou out of breath, when thou hast breath to say to me that thou art out of breath? Is thy news good or bad?

Nurse: (With a loud shriek) Lord, how my head aches! It beats as it would fall in twenty pieces! *(Juliet starts to rub the Nurse's head.)* My back! *(Juliet rubs her back.)* On t'other side! *(Juliet rubs the other side.)* Ah, my back, my back!

Juliet: In faith, I am sorry that thou art not well. Sweet, sweet Nurse, what says my love?

Nurse: (With kindness) Your love says, like an honest gentleman, and a courteous and a kind, and a handsome, and, I warrant, a virtuous . . . *(She looks around.)* Where is your mother?

Juliet: Where is my mother? *(She points at the door, frustrated.)* Why, she is within. Where should she be? How oddly thou repliest: "Your love says, like an honest gentleman, 'Where is your mother?'"

Nurse: (Pretending to be cross) O God's Lady dear! Is this the poultice for my aching bones? Henceforward do your messages yourself!

Juliet: (Coaxing) Come, what says Romeo?

Nurse: (With a big smile) Hie you hence to Friar Lawrence' cell. There stays a husband to make you a wife! *(Juliet hugs her, and the Nurse rises, hugging her back.)* Go! I'll to dinner. Hie you to the cell! *(She pushes her towards the door.)*

Juliet: Hie to high fortune! *(With a kiss)* Honest Nurse, farewell! *(She runs off, and the Nurse leaves, chuckling.)*

Announcer 1: At Friar Lawrence's cell, the lovers are married secretly.

(The servant brings on the cross banner. Romeo and the Friar enter from one side and Juliet from the other. Romeo carries some flowers for Juliet. The two lovers rush to each other to embrace, but the Friar firmly gets between them. He pushes them down to kneel on the floor and makes the Sign of the Cross over them.)

Friar: You shall not stay alone till Holy Church incorporate two in one!

(Then he has them rise. Romeo gives Juliet the flowers. Slowly the Friar leaves towards the church, and the lovers follow him, hand-in-hand.)

ACT III

Announcer 2: Since nobody else knows of Romeo and Juliet's wedding, life goes on as usual.

(Onto the stage stroll Benvolio and Mercutio, who hang up the street banner. They sprawl on the benches.)

Benvolio: I pray thee, good Mercutio, let's retire. The day is hot, the Capulets abroad, and, if we meet, we shall not escape a brawl. For now, these hot days, is the mad blood stirring. *(Mercutio yawns. Benvolio becomes alert, looking offstage.)* By my head, here comes the Capulets.

Mercutio: By my heel, I care not!

Tybalt: (Swaggering on, ready for a fight.) Gentlemen, a word with one of you.

Mercutio: (Ready to fight also) And but one word with one of us? Couple it with something—make it a word and a blow!

(Romeo enters, carrying a flower of Juliet's.)

Announcer 1: Tybalt still wants revenge on Romeo for going to the Capulet feast.

Tybalt: Here comes my man. *(He steps in front of Romeo.)* Romeo, thou art a villain!

Announcer 2: But Romeo knows that Tybalt is now his own cousin by marriage, and he is too happy to fight.

Romeo: (Gently) Tybalt, villain am I none. Therefore, farewell! *(He bows and starts to go.)*

Tybalt: Boy, this shall not excuse the injuries that thou hast done me. Therefore, turn and draw!

Romeo: I do protest I love thee better than thou canst devise. And so, good Capulet, be satisfied. *(He walks on. Mercutio is furious at the insult.)*

Mercutio: (To Romeo, for being cowardly.) O calm, dishonorable, vile submission! *(To Tybalt)* Will you pluck your sword out? Make haste!

(They fight. Romeo and Benvolio try to stop them.)

Romeo: Gentlemen, for shame! *(Trying to come between them.)* Tybalt, Mercutio . . . the Prince hath forbid bandying in Verona streets! *(Holding Mercutio's arm.)* Good Mercutio! *(Tybalt takes advantage of Romeo's interference and stabs Mercutio. Then he stops, stares, and runs away.)*

Mercutio: (Slowly, as he feels his death wound.) I am hurt. A plague on both your houses!

Romeo: Courage, man! The hurt cannot be much.

Mercutio: No, 'tis not so deep as a well, nor so wide as a church door, but 'tis enough. 'Twill serve. *(He makes a last joke.)* Ask for me tomorrow, and you shall find me a "grave" man. *(In anger)* A plague on both your houses! *(With desperate pleading to Romeo.)* Why the devil came you between us? I was hurt under your arm!

Romeo: Gentlemen, for shame!

Romeo: (Overcome with guilt) I thought all for the best.

Mercutio: Help me into some house, Benvolio, or I shall faint. *(He shouts out bitterly.)* A plague on both your houses! They have made worms' meat of me! *(Benvolio helps him go behind the curtains.)*

Romeo: (Looking at Juliet's flower) O sweet Juliet, thy beauty hath made me effeminate! *(He crushes it.)*

Benvolio: (Returning, sadly) O Romeo, Romeo! Brave Mercutio's dead! *(He looks offstage and says in shock.)* Here comes the furious Tybalt back again! *(Tybalt re-enters, ready to fight still more.)*

Romeo: (Drawing his sword in a rage.) Now, Tybalt, take the "villain" back again. *(He points to Heaven.)* For Mercutio's soul is but a little way above our heads. Either thou or I . . . or both . . . must go with him!

(They fight furiously, and Tybalt is slain. Romeo becomes dazed, seeing him sink to the ground. Benvolio pushes Romeo off as people gather.)

Benvolio: Romeo, away, be gone! The Prince will doom thee death if thou art taken. Be gone, away!

Romeo: (In misery over his bad luck.) O, I am Fortune's fool! *(He rushes off.)*

(The Prince enters, with the Capulets.)

Prince: Where are the vile beginners of this fray?

Benvolio: O noble Prince, . . . *(He points to Tybalt.)* . . . there lies the man, slain by young Romeo, that slew thy kinsman, brave Mercutio.

Lady Capulet: (Kneeling by Tybalt) Tybalt, my cousin! O my brother's child! O Prince, Romeo must not live!

Announcer 1: The Prince sentences Romeo, not to death but to exile or banishment. If he stays in the city, he must die.

Prince: (Giving judgment) And for that offence, immediately we do exile him hence. Let Romeo hence in haste, else, when he's found, that hour is his last. *(To his guards)* Bear hence this body.

(As all leave sadly, a servant enters with Juliet's banner. Juliet follows, looking romantically at the sky.)

Announcer 2: That evening, Juliet waits for her young husband.

Juliet: Come, gentle night. Come, loving, black-browed night. Give me my Romeo! *(She smiles at a fanciful thought.)* And when he shall die, take him and cut him out in little stars. And he will make the face of heaven so fine that all the world will be in love with night! *(The Nurse enters, weeping.)* Now, Nurse, what news?

Nurse: (Sitting) Tybalt is gone, and Romeo banished. Romeo that killed him—he is banished!

Juliet: O God! Did Romeo's hand shed Tybalt's blood?

Nurse: It did, it did! Alas the day, it did! *(Juliet bursts into tears.)* I'll find Romeo to comfort you. *(Kindly)* Your Romeo will be here at night! I'll to him. He is hid at Lawrence' cell.

Juliet: O, find him! And bid him come to take his last farewell.

(She leaves sadly, and the Nurse bustles out the opposite direction. A servant replaces the banner with the Friar's cross. The Friar enters.)

Announcer 1: At the Friar's, Romeo waits in hiding.

Friar:(Calling) Romeo, come forth, thou fearful man!

Romeo: *(Entering)* Father, what news?

Friar: Hence from Verona art thou . . . banished!

Romeo: *(Slowly)* There is no world without Verona walls. Heaven is here, where Juliet lives. And every cat and dog and little mouse live here in Heaven and may look on her. But Romeo may not. O Friar! *(He collapses on the ground in tears.)*

Friar: *(As he hears a knock.)* Hark, how they knock! *(He tries to rouse Romeo.)* Run to my study! *(He goes to the door. The Nurse appears.)*

Nurse: I come from Lady Juliet.

Romeo: How is it with her? Doth not she think me an old murderer? Where is she? And how doth she?

Nurse: O, she says nothing, but weeps and weeps.

Friar: (To Romeo) Art thou a man? Thy tears are womanish! *(Patting his shoulder.)* What, rouse thee, man! Thy Juliet is alive. *(He pushes Romeo towards the door.)* Go, get thee to thy love.

Announcer 2: The Friar warns Romeo to leave Juliet's chamber early next morning and go to the city of Mantua.

Announcer 1: There he will have to stay until the Friar announces the marriage and gets the Prince to pardon him.

Friar: But look thou stay not till the watch be set, for then thou canst not pass to Mantua, where thou shalt live till we can find a time to blaze your marriage, beg pardon of the Prince and . . . call thee back! *(He gives Romeo a hug.)*

Romeo: (Half-smiling as he leaves.) Farewell! *(The others follow. The Capulet banner is hung.)*

Announcer 2: Meanwhile, to cheer up Juliet, because he thinks she is weeping for her cousin Tybalt's death, Lord Capulet decides to have her marry young Count Paris right away.

(Capulet, Lady Capulet and Paris enter.)

Capulet: (To Paris) Look you, she loved her kinsman Tybalt dearly, and so did I. *(He sighs.)* Wife, go to her ere you go to bed. Acquaint her here of my son Paris' love. *(He stops with an idea.)* But soft, what day is this?

Paris: Monday, my lord.

Capulet: Monday! Ha, ha! Well, Wednesday is too soon. On Thursday let it be! On Thursday, tell her, she shall be married to this noble earl. *(He smiles at Paris.)* But what say you to Thursday?

Paris: (Overjoyed) My lord, I would that Thursday were tomorrow!

Capulet: (To his astonished wife) Go you to Juliet! Prepare her, wife, against this wedding day. *(To Paris, showing him to the door.)* Farewell, my lord! *(They leave.)*

Announcer 1: The next morning at dawn, Romeo leaves his young bride. *(The orchard banner is hung.)*

(Romeo and Juliet appear above, on her balcony.)

Juliet: Wilt thou be gone? It is not yet near day.

Romeo: (Pointing to the sky. The stars are gone.) Look, love, night's candles are burnt out, and jocund day stands tiptoe on the misty mountaintops. I must be gone and live, or stay and die!

Juliet: Yond light is not daylight. Therefore, stay yet. *(She holds him back from leaving.)*

Romeo: (Pretending to give in to her.) Let me be taken. Let me be put to death. I have more care to stay than will to go. Come, Death, and welcome!

Juliet: (Sadly pushing him away.) Hie hence, be gone, away! More light and light it grows!

Romeo: More light and light. More dark and dark our woes!

Nurse: (Calling) Madam, your lady mother is coming to your chamber. The day is broke!

Romeo: Farewell, farewell! One kiss and I'll descend. *(He kisses her lightly and goes down to the ground, where he waves to her.)* Farewell!

Juliet: Either my eyesight fails, or thou lookest pale.

Romeo: Dry sorrow drinks our blood. Adieu, adieu!

(He runs off. She descends from the balcony. Juliet's chamber banner is hung.)

Announcer 2: So the lovers have to part. And Juliet must pretend the wedding never took place.

(Onto the stage comes Lady Capulet, calling. The Nurse follows her.)

Lady Capulet: Ho, daughter, are you up?

Juliet: (Entering) Who is it that calls? *(She wipes the tears from her eyes.)*

Lady Capulet: (Misunderstanding the tears) Evermore weeping for your cousin's death?

Juliet: I cannot choose but ever weep the friend.

Lady Capulet: But now I'll tell thee joyful tidings, girl.

Juliet: And joy comes well in such a needful time.

Lady Capulet: Marry, my child, early next Thursday morn, the gallant, young and noble gentleman, the County Paris, at Saint Peter's Church, shall happily make thee there . . . a joyful bride!

Juliet: (Horrified) Now, by Saint Peter's Church and Peter too, he shall not make me there a joyful bride! I pray you, tell my lord and father, madam, I will not marry yet.

Lady Capulet: (Crossly) Here comes your father. Tell him so yourself.

Capulet: (Entering, smiling broadly) How now, wife? Have you delivered to her our decree?

Lady Capulet: (Scornful of Juliet) Ay, sir, but she will none. She gives you thanks!

Capulet: (Growing more and more angry as he speaks.) How? Will she none? Is she not proud? *(He shakes his fist at her.)* Mistress minion you, thank me no thankings, nor proud me no prouds. *(He begins to shout.)* But fettle your fine joints against Thursday next to go with Paris to Saint Peter's Church! Disobedient wretch!

Lady Capulet: (Trying to calm him.) You are too hot!

Capulet: It makes me mad! *(To Juliet)* Look to it . . . think on it . . . Thursday is near. And you be mine, I'll give you to my friend. And you be not . . . hang, beg, starve, die in the street! Bethink you! *(He stamps off, furious.)*

Lady Capulet: (To Juliet) Talk not to me, for I'll not speak a word. I have done with thee! *(She sweeps off also, cold and disapproving.)*

Announcer 1: Juliet turns to her best friend, the Nurse, for help. But the Nurse does not give very good advice.

Juliet: O Nurse, how shall this be prevented? *(The Nurse hugs her and thinks very hard.)*

Nurse: Faith, here it is. Romeo is banished. *(Brightly)* Then, I think it best you married with the county. O, he's a lovely gentleman! Romeo's a dishcloth to him! *(Juliet looks shocked and draws away.)*

Announcer 2: But Juliet would rather die than commit bigamy. Her one hope now is the kind old Friar.

Juliet: (Coldly) Well, thou has comforted me marvelous much. Go in, and tell my lady I am gone to Lawrence' cell, to make confession.

Nurse: (Full of smiles) Marry, I will, and this is wisely done! *(She leaves happily.)*

Juliet: (Looking after her.) O most wicked counselor! *(With determination.)* I'll to the Friar to know his remedy. *(Putting a dagger in her belt.)* If all else fail, myself have power to die! *(She goes.)*

ACT IV

Announcer 1: At Friar Lawrence's cell, the County Paris makes wedding arrangements, to the old Friar's surprise and alarm.

(A servant carries on the Cross banner, and as he leaves, Friar Lawrence and Paris enter.)

Friar: On Thursday, sir? The time is very short.

Paris: My father Capulet will have it so.

Friar: You say you do not know the lady's mind? *(He frowns.)* I like it not. *(Glancing offstage)* Look, sir, here comes the lady toward my cell.

(Juliet enters in a rush but stops short when she sees Paris.)

Paris: (Smiling) Happily met, my lady and my wife!

Juliet: (Ignoring him) Are you at leisure, holy father, now?

Friar: (Pushing Paris out the door.) My lord, we must entreat the time alone. *(Paris bows to Juliet and leaves. Juliet rushes to the Friar, who holds her and pats her back like a child.)*

Juliet: Come weep with me . . . past hope, past cure, past help!

Friar: O, Juliet, I already know thy grief. I hear thou must, on Thursday next, be married to this county.

Juliet: (Desperately) If, in thy wisdom, thou canst give no help, . . . *(She draws her dagger.)* . . . with this knife, I'll help it presently. *(The Friar takes the knife away from her, shaking his head.)*

Announcer 2: The Friar has another plan. Juliet must take one of his medicines, a sleeping potion.

Friar: Hold, daughter. I do spy a kind of hope. *(He goes to the side of the stage and returns with a little vial or bottle with a cork.)* Go home, be merry, consent to marry Paris.

Wednesday is tomorrow. Tomorrow night look that thou lie alone. Let not thy nurse lie with thee in thy chamber. Take thou this vial . . . *(He gives it to her.)* . . . being then in bed, and this distilled liquor drink thou off. *(She nods with understanding as the Friar continues mysteriously.)*

When presently through all thy veins shall run a cold humor. The roses in thy lips and cheeks shall fade. Each part shall appear like death. And in this "death" thou shalt continue two-and-forty hours, and then awake as from a pleasant sleep.

Announcer 1: The Friar will write Romeo to come. And when Juliet wakes, Romeo will take her to Mantua to live.

Friar: In the meantime, shall Romeo by my letters know our drift, and hither shall he come. And he and I will watch thy waking. And that very night shall Romeo bear thee hence . . . to Mantua!

Juliet: Love, give me strength! *(She kisses his old cheek.)* Farewell, dear father! *(She runs out the door. He leaves in the other direction.)*

Announcer 2: Juliet returns home to follow the Friar's instructions. She agrees to marry Paris.

(Onto the stage comes a servant with the Capulet banner. He is followed by the Nurse, Lady Capulet and Capulet.)

Capulet: *(Giving a list to the servant.)* So many guests invite as here are writ. *(The servant bows and leaves. Capulet speaks to the Nurse.)* What, is my daughter gone to Friar Lawrence?

Nurse: *(Looking offstage)* See where she comes from shrift with merry look.

Juliet: *(Kneeling before her father with a smile.)* I have learnt me to repent the sin of disobedient opposition to you. Pardon, I beseech you!

Capulet: *(Joyfully)* Send for the county. *(With an inspiration to make the wedding earlier.)* I'll have this knot knit up tomorrow morning!

Lady Capulet: No, not till Thursday! There is time enough!

Capulet: (Roaring happily) We'll to church tomorrow! My heart is wondrous light! *(He hurries them away.)*

Announcer 1: That night Juliet prepares to take the sleeping potion.

(The servant brings on Juliet's banner and parts the center curtains, showing the end of Juliet's bed. Juliet, her mother, and the Nurse enter.)

Juliet: (To her mother) So please you, let me now be left alone, and let the Nurse this night sit up with you. For I am sure you have your hands full all in this so-sudden business! *(The older women look surprised and pleased at her cooperation.)*

Lady Capulet: (With a little kiss.) Good night! Get thee to bed and rest. *(She and the Nurse leave.)*

Juliet: (Calling after them softly) Farewell! God knows when we shall meet again. *(She takes the vial out of her pocket.)* My dismal scene I needs must act alone. *(Her fears begin to mount.)*

What if this mixture do not work at all? What if it be a poison? How if, when I am laid into the tomb, I wake before the time that Romeo come? Shall I not then be stifled in the vault, to whose foul mouth no healthsome air breathes in, and there die strangled?

Or if I live, is it not very like that I, so early waking, run mad? *(She thinks she sees Tybalt's ghost walking.)* O, look! Methinks I see my cousin's ghost seeking out Romeo. *(She puts out her hands to keep it off.)* Stay, Tybalt, stay!

(She sits on the bed, sobbing. Then she lifts the vial to her lips.) Romeo, I come! This do I drink to thee! *(She drinks and then slowly lies down on the bed, as sleep comes over her.)*

Announcer 2: The night passes quickly, and the Nurse comes for Juliet, to dress her for church.

Nurse: (Calling, as she comes in happily.) Mistress! What, Juliet! *(She shakes her head.)* Why, lamb! Why, lady! Fie, you slugabed. *(She frowns.)* How sound is she asleep! I must needs wake her. *(She goes to the bed and shakes her.)* Lady! Lady! Lady! *(With growing horror, she backs away.)* Help, help! My lady's . . . dead!

(Her screams bring on Lord and Lady Capulet.)

Lady Capulet: What is the matter?

Nurse: Look, look! *(She points at the bed.)*

Lady Capulet: O me, O me! My child, my only life! *(She takes the girl in her arms.)*

Capulet: (Brushing his wife aside) Ha! Let me see her. *(He takes her pulse.)* She's cold, her blood is settled and her joints are stiff. *(Gently he kisses her and pulls the sheet over her face.)* Death lies on her like an untimely frost upon the sweetest flower of all the field.

Nurse: O lamentable day!

Lady Capulet: O woeful time!

Capulet: Death ties up my tongue and will not let me speak. *(The Friar and Paris enter, smiling.)*

Friar: Come, is the bride ready to go to church?

Capulet: Ready to go, but never to return. *(To Paris)* Death is my son-in-law. My daughter he hath wedded. Life, living—all is Death's. *(Paris kneels by Juliet's bed.)*

Friar: (Giving comfort that Juliet is in Heaven.) Peace, ho, for shame! Heaven and yourself had part in this fair maid. Now Heaven hath all. And all the better is it for the maid. Dry up your tears and bear her to church.

Capulet: (Giving sad orders) All things that we ordained festival . . . turn from their office to black funeral: our instruments to melancholy bells, our wedding cheer to a sad burial feast. Our bridal flowers serve for a burial corpse, and all things change them to the contrary.

Friar: (Urging all to leave) Sir, go you in. And madam. And go, Sir Paris. Everyone prepare to follow this fair corpse unto her grave. *(As the others leave, he first takes the vial from Juliet's hand secretly. Then he pushes Juliet's cot back and closes the curtains on it before he, too, leaves.)*

ACT V

Announcer 1: The Friar writes Romeo of Juliet's pretended death. But the messenger is delayed, and the letter never arrives.

(Romeo strolls on stage and sits, looking happily into the sky. A servant hangs the Mantua banner.)

Announcer 2: So in Mantua, the banished Romeo knows nothing of the Friar's plans. Romeo has had a dream about good news, and he feels lighthearted.

Romeo: My dreams presage some joyful news at hand. My bosom's lord sits lightly in his throne! I dreamt my lady came and found me dead, and breathed such life with kisses in my lips that I revived and was an Emperor! *(He laughs easily at the idea.)*

(Seeing his servant Balthasar enter, he turns to greet him.) News from Verona! How now, Balthasar? How doth my lady? Is my father well? How fares my Juliet? That I ask again, for nothing can be ill if she be well.

Balthasar: *(Sadly)* Then she is well, and nothing can be ill. *(He takes off his hat and crosses himself.)* Her body sleeps in Capel's monument. *(He points to Heaven.)* And her immortal part with angels lives. *(With a harsh cry)* O, pardon me for bringing these ill news!

Romeo: (Slowly he rises, stunned.) Is it even so? *(For a long moment he is silent. Slowly he shakes his fist at Heaven and shouts.)* Then I defy you, stars! *(To Balthasar, quickly)* Get me post horses. I will hence tonight! *(The servant bows and leaves. Romeo speaks to himself in a quiet voice.)* Well, Juliet, I will lie with thee tonight.

Announcer 1: Since he thinks Juliet is dead, Romeo decides to die with her. He visits a poor apothecary, who sells drugs and poisons.

Romeo: (Looking around) I do remember an apothecary, and hereabouts he dwells. And in his needy shop a tortoise hung, an alligator stuffed, and other skins of ill-shaped fishes. To myself I said, "And if a man did need a poison now, here lives a wretch would sell it him." As I remember, this should be the house. *(He parts the curtains.)* What, ho! Apothecary!

Apothecary: (Putting his head out, a thin, starved man) Who calls so loud?

Romeo: I see that thou art poor. *(He shows him a bag of gold.)* There is forty ducats. Let me have a dram of poison.

Apothecary: (With fear) Such mortal drugs I have, but Mantua's law is death.

Romeo: Famine is in thy cheeks. *(He rattles the gold.)*

Apothecary: (Reluctantly) My poverty, but not my will, consents.

Romeo: I pay thy poverty and not thy will.

Apothecary: (Looking about uneasily, he gives Romeo a little vial of poison.) Put this in any liquid thing and drink it off.

Romeo: (Handing him the money) There is thy gold. Farewell. *(The apothecary snatches the gold and goes behind the curtains. Romeo leaves hurriedly.)*

Announcer 2: That night, Juliet is placed in her tomb. Paris comes to put flowers on the grave of his bride.

(A servant places the tomb banner by the curtains, which will be the door to the tomb.)

Paris: (Entering with a page) Hence, and stand aloof. Whistle, as signal that thou hearest something approach. Give me those flowers. Do as I bid thee, go. *(The page bows and hides to one side.)*

(Paris kneels at the curtains and places the flowers on the ground.) Sweet flower, with flowers thy bridal bed I strew. *(The page whistles a signal, and Paris rises and stands to one side.)*

Romeo: (Entering with Balthasar) Give me the wrenching iron. *(Balthasar hands him a crowbar. Romeo gives him a note.)* Hold, take this letter. Early in the morning see thou deliver it to my father. Hence, be gone!

Balthasar: (To himself) For all this same, I'll hide me hereabout. *(He hides and watches Romeo pry at the center curtain.)*

Paris: *(Drawing his sword and going to Romeo.)* Stop, vile Montague! Condemned villain, obey and go with me, for thou must die!

Romeo: Good gentle youth, tempt not a desperate man!

Paris: *(Trying to arrest Romeo)* I do apprehend thee for a felon here! *(They cross swords.)*

Page: O Lord, they fight! I will go call the watch. *(He runs off.)*

(Romeo and Paris fight back and forth, but Paris is no match for Romeo's desperate fury. Romeo soon lunges and Paris falls to the ground, wounded.)

Paris: O, I am slain! If thou be merciful, open the tomb, lay me with Juliet. *(He dies.)*

Romeo: In faith, I will! *(He looks closely at the dead man.)* Noble County Paris! *(Shaking his head, as if confused.)* What said my man? I think he told me Paris should have married Juliet. *(He takes the unlucky Paris's hand.)* O, give me thy hand, one writ with me in sour misfortune's book!

(He opens the curtains to show Juliet on her tomb, covered with a veil of lace.)

Announcer 1: In the tomb, Romeo says farewell to his bride.

Romeo: O my love, my wife! *(He folds back the veil to see her face.)* Death hath had no power yet upon

Romeo: Here's to my love!

thy beauty. Why art thou yet so fair? *(He looks around.)* I still will stay with thee, and never from this palace of dim night depart again. Here will I set up my everlasting rest.

Eyes, look your last! *(He raises her slightly and holds her to his heart.)* Arms, take your last embrace. And lips, seal with a righteous kiss a dateless bargain to engrossing death! *(He kisses her gently and puts her down on the tomb.)*

(Taking out the vial of poison, he holds it up like a toast.) Here's to my love! *(He drinks it and immediately feels the effects.)* O true apothecary! Thy drugs are quick. Thus with a kiss I die! *(He kisses her and sinks to the floor beside the tomb.)*

(For a moment all is quiet. Juliet stirs a little in her sleep. Then Friar Lawrence enters with a crowbar also.)

Friar: Fear comes upon me. *(Calling)* Romeo! *(He sees Paris and the bloody swords.)* Alack, alack, what blood is this? *(He discovers the bodies.)* Romeo! O pale! *(Looking at the other corpse.)* Who else? What, Paris too? *(Juliet starts to waken.)* The lady stirs!

Juliet: *(Rising a little and smiling.)* O comfortable Friar! Where is my lord? I do remember well where I should be, and there I am. Where is my Romeo? *(She glances around a little.)*

Friar: (Listening to some faraway shouts.) I hear some noise. Lady, come from that nest of death. Come, come away. *(She looks confused and he points out Romeo's body. She is frozen in grief.)* Thy husband there lies dead. And Paris too. *(She bites her lip.)* Come, go, good Juliet! I dare no longer stay! *(He runs off.)*

Announcer 2: Juliet realizes Romeo has died only a few minutes before. She wants to join him in death.

Juliet: (Getting off the bed and kneeling by Romeo's body.) What's here? A cup, closed in my true-love's hand? Poison, I see, hath been his timeless end. *(She tries to drink from it, but it is empty. She turns it upside-down and shakes it sadly.)* O churl! Drunk all and left no friendly drop to help me after? I will kiss thy lips. Haply some poison yet doth hang on them.

(She kisses him and draws back with new sorrow, realizing he has just died.) Thy lips are warm!

Watchman: (Offstage) Lead, boy. Which way?

Juliet: (Alarmed) Yea, noise? Then I'll be brief. *(She finds Romeo's dagger.)* O happy dagger! *(She holds it to her heart.)* This is thy sheath—there rust, and let me die . . . *(She stabs herself and falls across Romeo's body.)*

(The page enters with the watchman, the Prince, the Capulets and Lord Montague, with Friar Lawrence. The Prince looks at the bodies first.)

Capulet: O Heavens! O wife, look how our daughter bleeds!

Lady Capulet: O me!

Prince: Come, Montague . . . *(He points to the dead lovers.)*

Montague: (Not seeing them at first.) Alas, my liege, my wife is dead tonight! What further woe conspires against mine age? O . . . *(He sees his dead son and kneels, praying.)*

Prince: (Motioning to the watchman) Bring forth the parties of suspicion.

Friar: (Coming forward) I am the greatest! *(He strikes his fist upon his chest with shame.)*

Prince: Then say at once what thou dost know in this.

Friar: I will be brief. Romeo, there dead, was husband to that Juliet. I married them. Then gave I her a sleeping potion. But when I came, here lay the noble Paris and true Romeo dead. She, too desperate, would not go with me. *(He turns away, weeping.)*

Prince: (Sternly, to the two fathers.) Where be these enemies? *(The fathers face each other.)* Capulet, Montague, Heaven finds means to kill your joys with love!

Announcer 1: Over the bodies of their dead children, Capulet and Montague declare peace.

Capulet: (Slowly holding forth his hand in friendship.) O brother Montague, give me thy hand. No more can I demand. *(The two old fathers clasp hands.)*

Announcer 2: Only one thing more can the fathers do—put up gold statues of their dead children.

Montague: But I can give thee more. For I will raise her statue in pure gold, that while Verona by that name is known, there shall no figure at such rate be set as that of true and faithful Juliet!

Capulet: As rich shall Romeo by his lady lie—poor sacrifices of our enmity. *(They weep together.)*

Prince: (Looking at the gray morning sky.) A glooming peace this morning with it brings. The sun for sorrow will not show his head. Go hence, to have more talk of these sad things. Some shall be pardoned, and some punished. For never was a story of more woe . . . than this of Juliet and her Romeo. *(They pull the curtains across the figures of the dead lovers and leave slowly to the sound of sad music. The announcers follow.)*

The End